1

Place of the Stingray is a very special place on the Limestone Coast of South Australia. It has been important to the Boandik people for thousands of years. It is also known as The Caves.

Knowledge Books and Software

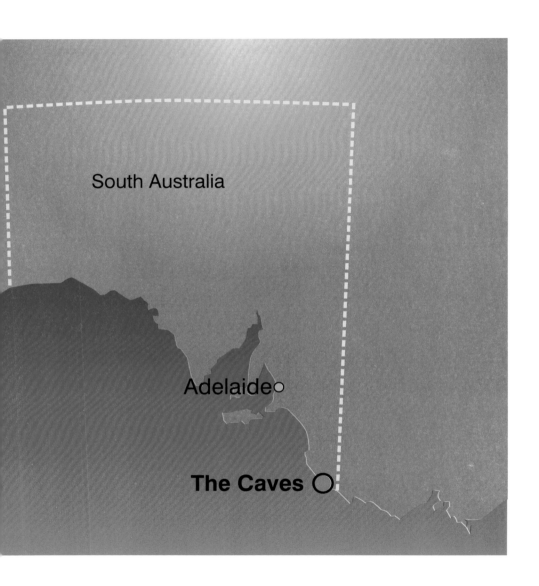

South Australia

Adelaide ○

The Caves ○

3

The Boandik people lived here for thousands of years. They lived off the food from the sea. Many of them hunted the stingray, which is how the place got its name. The ocean had more than enough food for everyone.

4

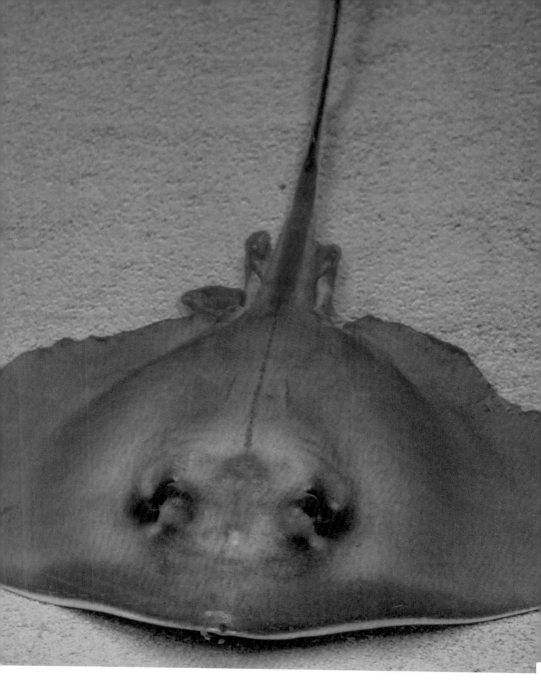

5

Knowledge Books and Software

Lobster and abalone were hunted and seaweed was eaten. Cockles and whelks were collected off the rocks. The lakes and land provided lots of food. Eels and freshwater fish were caught and bird's eggs were collected. Fruit and yams were also gathered.

Knowledge Books and Software

7

For many years, the Boandik people lived peacefully here. They looked after their land and ocean, only taking what they needed. However, things started to change in the early 1800's. Whalers and sealers arrived from other countries and hunted along the coast. Other settlers then arrived and started grazing cattle and sheep.

Knowledge Books and Software

9

This caused many problems for the Boandik people. They could no longer hunt in some of their favourite grounds. Cattle and sheep ate all the grass. This meant that the native animals had to move to other areas to find food. Waterholes were spoiled, taking away more of their food sources.

Knowledge Books and Software

11

The settlers also brought dangerous diseases with them, like the common cold and smallpox. These diseases killed many Europeans. They also killed many Boandik people. All of these things made life very difficult for these proud peoples.

Knowledge Books and Software

13

The Boandik people realised that the settlers' sheep were easy to hunt. They did not think they were doing anything wrong. This is the way they had found their food and survived for thousands of years. However, they were accused of stealing.

Knowledge Books and Software

Angry settlers rounded up many of the Boandik families. They pushed them out of their peaceful camps. They forced them through the coastal bush and up over the cliff. They had no choice but to jump into the ocean where many of them drowned.

Knowledge Books and Software

17

However, legend says that some survived by swimming into an underwater cave. This cave had a trapped air pocket which allowed them to breathe. These caves could not be seen from land. When darkness fell, some of these brave Boandik people emerged from the water and climbed back to land to safely escape.

18

19

Today, people visit The Caves to honour the brave, determined people who survived. Their brave actions ensured that this is still a very special Boandik place today.

Knowledge Books and Software

21

Surveys have been completed in the area to help protect this important place. Many stone artefacts have been found by researchers. These were used by the Boandik people thousands of years ago. The Caves is considered an important historical site to all Australians today. We must continue to protect it for our future generations.

23

Word bank

special

Boandik

abalone

cockles

whelks

freshwater

peacefully

favourite

waterholes

sources

dangerous

smallpox

difficult

accused

underwater

emerged

honour

determined

continued

ensured

artefacts

researchers

historical

generations

Knowledge Books and Software